The Fourth Symphony

A symphony in words

By Wolf Larsen

For Phil & Leo

ABOUT WOLF LARSEN

Wolf Larsen is a comedian, writer, and poet who has traveled through over 50 countries. Wolf worked for years as a seasonal laborer in Alaska. His fiction and poetry has been published in literary magazines around the world.

Other Books by Wolf Larsen

Capitalism Sucks (non-fiction)

Honky Fucking Crazy N-Word Lover (a novel)

Pricks, Cunts, & Motherfuckers: The Novel About New York City

Eulogy for the Human Race (poems)

Pornography (poems)

Penis! Penis!! Penis!!! (a play)

Ten Thousand Penises in Your Ear (a novel)

There are many other books by Wolf Larsen to choose from. Most of Wolf's books can be purchased at online retailers.

The Fourth Symphony

By Wolf Larsen

As the nuclear missiles fly across the world the violins play. As the mushroom clouds erupt across the Earth the violins play. As all of humanity screeches with terror the violins play.

The cellos play with so much darkness... So much darkness... So much darkness...

The clarinet summons the night to begin for forever. The flute cries with so many tears. The oboe sings the eulogy of billions of people...

The violins play all the storms Screeching across the world. The cellos play so much thunder, so much thunder...

The violins begin plucking the sky with so much rain... So much rain... The violins play the rain falling upon the ruins of the world. The cellos play a nostalgia for a world that used to exist. The double basses play a darkness that will never end.

All the woodwinds screech with so much terror. All the woodwinds screech with so much Night & day clashing with each other... All the woodwinds screech & screech & screech...

And the brass section joins with all the screeching. The trumpet does a Nightmare on a beautiful sunny day. The French horn sounds out a Long dark scream. All the trombones are rE-cReaTinG oUr bRaiNs & Re-crEatiNg ouR brAinS...

And the tuba tries to tell a joke... But the harp plays a Happy man swallowed by sadness. The harp is playing with so much Sunshine in the Pussy. And the cellos join in with lots of Pussy flying everywhere...

The violins play storm after storm of circus clowns jumping off of people's heads. The violins play the winds of Other lands arriving at your doorstep. The violins make the seas become crazy...

And the cellos begin marching... The cellos begin marching off to Places that don't exist yet... The cellos are marching off to Paintings that are being created in your mind...

And the clarinet does a Comedian kidnapped by space aliens. And the oboe does lots of Fuzzy stuff growing everywhere. And the flute plays a symphony on 10,000 other planets at the same time...

And then all the trombones go for a walk in a dream full of strawberries. And the tuba goes for a swim in the reader's mind. And the trumpet discovers 100 clones of the reader standing outside of the reader's door. The trumpet is playing so much Charles Manson...

And the music sounds like a holiday spent at the Charles Manson resort in outer space, it sounds like Your baby playing with a dozen chainsaws, the music sounds like so much Meowing cats being devoured by the English language...

And the female singer sings: "I have Music with so many herpes sores all over it for you!"

And the flute accompanies her with a
Right hook onto the chin...

And the male singer sings: "Give me
your diseases of music sick music! Give
me your Vagina full of music! Give me a
trip to every planet in your head where
there's music!"

And all the instruments in the orchestra
leap up into a Cambodian genocide. And
the entire orchestra is playing a Bunch of
circus clowns performing comedy at the
Jonestown massacre. And the orchestra
is playing Thousands of Salvador Dali
clones all stabbing & stabbing each
other. And it sounds like a circus with
lots of cyanide. It all sounds like so Much
space aliens tapping out beats in the
bedroom...

And then the flute does a Trip to 6000
brains on fire, and while the flute plays,

the female singer sings: "I smile at the Universe on fire! I smile at all the musical fires burning in our Yearning desires!"

And the trumpet does so much Frogs on lily pads floating above your head, and while the trumpet plays, the male singer sings: "I was in a dark dungeon of music once, where the musical notes became human faces! And the mUsiCaL-nOte-hUmAn-fAcEs kept screaming & screaming at me All night long!"

And then the entire chorus of men & women sing together: "We are in a nation where all government business is conducted in music! We are in a universe where everyone's skin is contaminated with music! We are in a time where all the animals sing to us in collages & tornadoes & earthquakes of music! And we sing music as we make love! We sing music as we die!"

And that's when the entire orchestra goes wild with Temptation! The orchestra goes wild with Sexual juices! All the instruments are playing so much sexual juices & more sexual juices & more sexual juices!

And then all is silence...

And now the Harp plays so much Death so softly. And the flute joins in, and the flute does a Dance around death. And the oboe joins in too, and the oboe plays lots of Death worship...

And then the violins leap forward into a frenzy a tornado a psycho cat fight. And the cellos go backwards into a whirlpool of sadism. And the double basses go up & down with lots of Rough seas...

And the brass section leaps up with a Manic lust.

And then the woodwinds all jump in with so much Dick & Pussy...

And the timpani drums are doing so much Cocaine that the music bursts with heart attacks & lust & violence.

And the trumpet shouts out a Welcome to all the cannibals to join the festivities.

Then all is silent again...

The flute plays Your mother going insane...

The female singer sings: "Insanity is a blessing from the Goddess of Creativity! Insanity is a curse of poetry & music & art swimming around you all day & night! Insanity is endless tornadoes of creation all Descending on your brains all the time!"

And the singer's voice sounds like a trip
to Mars. Her voice sounds like Somebody
cutting themselves over & over again
with a razor blade. Her voice sounds like
so much Cat fights between two women
scratching up each other's faces & pulling
each other's hair.

And the trumpet plays lots of
Celebrations of poetry & music dancing
through all our orgasms & orgies!

And the male singer sings: "Celebrate
the Songs of sin! Celebrate the musical
Penis that conquers the silence!
Celebrate the Singing hookers of that
bordello in Avignon, who sing out of that
painting with so much Forever!"

And his voice sounds like the happiest
cannibalism that you have ever heard!
His voice sounds like Hundreds of wild

animals. His voice sounds like so much Explosions in outer space...

And then the entire orchestra plays Hundreds of colorful butterflies flying in the air above the heads of the audience members... And the music sounds like All the world's punk rockers committing homicide & suicide at the same time. It all sounds like a thousand poisonous snakes slithering along the floor...

And the entire chorus sings together: "Poison us with Your words! Poison us with Your music! Poison us with Your art!"

And then the ondes Martenot starts to play Your brain splattered on canvases across the world... And the Erie & spooky sounds of the ondes Martenot fly across the room like Musical bats singing All their diseases to you. The music is flying everywhere! The ondes Martenot sounds like a Halloween party with naked people from every century of human history! The ondes Martenot sounds like Your children suddenly turning into space aliens! And the ondes Martenot sounds like All the ghosts of Treblinka!

And then the violins jump in with a Thunderstorm... And the violins are playing so much Rain that all the towns near & far are being drowned by musical notes. And the violins are Dancing the rhythms all the way to some impossible place that doesn't exist yet.

And then the cellos jump in with a science-fiction adventure. And the cellos are playing Pornographic science fiction adventures in ancient Rome...

And the double basses enter with a Sudden car crash...

And then all the strings together start playing All the women from all the whorehouses near & far walking naked into the symphony. They're playing politics with lots of cum. They're playing So much hunger that empty bellies are exploding everywhere. And all the strings together sound like You & all your relatives snorting cocaine together! It all sounds like the cocaine growing in the fields of South America are singing to you!

And then the ondes Martenot jumps in again! And once again, the sounds of the ondes Martenot are flying across the auditorium. The ondes Martenot sounds like Halloween having anal sex with Christmas! It sounds like Lots of orgies in your food! The music flying everywhere like musical Vaginas & musical Penises flying into your daydreams!

And then the voices of the chorus rise like a giant revolution! The chorus rises like a revolt! All the voices of the chorus sounds like a sea of Endless people rising up into a giant fist!

And the chorus sings: "Let's revolt with Our voices! Let's revolt with so much Thunder! We will revolt like Seas of anger that suddenly arise and swallow Everything!"

And the ondes Martenot begins flying its music across the auditorium again. The music is flying around like Space satellites on crack-cocaine! So much music making so much Destruction! The ondes Martenot sounding like So many octopuses flying through the air above everyone's heads!

And that's when the entire brass section opens up with a New century of Wishes!

The entire brass section together playing so much Artificial intelligence devouring the human race! The brass section playing more Bouncing testicles and more Bouncing testicles and more Bouncing testicles...

And then the entire woodwind section begins disco dancing the Italian Renaissance! And the woodwind section blows lots of bullet holes through all the formality & decorum! And the woodwind section Sends all the astronauts in outer space into Your bedroom, where they float through all the galaxies crashing out of your Vagina!

And then all is silence...

And the harp is playing You having a nervous breakdown... The harp sounds like Nuclear bombs quietly going off in your head... The harp is creating an empty world where nothing remains...

And the female singer sings: "And the empty world creeps around the Music, and the music creeps around the empty world! It's an empty world full of cockroaches devouring us! It's a place where the musical notes search for people's ears but can't find any Ears to listen!"

And the flute plays Your mother breast-feeding you... And the voice of the flute is like Your mother's voice. And the voice of the flute is something so pure... And the flute's voice is Searching for all your happy memories.

And the male singer sings: "I am the male version of your mother! I got lost somewhere between my childhood & my old age! I'm not myself anymore, and I can't find the way back to myself!"

And the clarinet jumps in with a naughty chase of musical notes across the pages. And the clarinet plays two happy kids playing in a field of Corpses. And the voice of the clarinet is like Endless happy frogs invading the planet Mars. And the clarinet creates a happy reader smiling all the way to his old age...

And then the ondes Martenot jumps in again and creates a bunch of Beautiful nightmares for everybody. The ondes Martenot creates so much purple & more purple & more purple. The ondes Martenot is a wild Monster that wants to eat you!

And the timpani drums join the ondes Martenot. And together the timpani drums & the ondes Martenot sound like so much Racial tension on the streets of America. Together, the timpani drums & the ondes Martenot create so many humans screeching a paradise of words! They create so much Peanut butter & jelly feelings in outer space! The sounds in the auditorium are a deafening civil war Of frogs & more frogs & more frogs...

And then the violins join the timpani drums & ondes Martenot. And the violins are Trampling all over a landscape of Bright colors. And the violins are Traveling back and forth between the moment that the human race was born, and the Moment the human race will be extinct. And the violins are Creating so many words that are creating so many eulogies for the human race.

And then all is silence...

And the male singer sings: "I am a bullet through your Daydreams!"

And the entire chorus sings: "I am a storm Laughing through your entire life!"

And the female singer sings: "I am Waterfalls of rage Crashing down upon each & every one of your days!"

And the entire chorus sings: "We are the happiness of immaculate conception in the orgies of Strangers! And we are the unhappiness of time slowly gnawing away at your body!"

And then the ondes Martenot jumps Up again and creates a bunch of Silliness erupting everywhere! And the ondes Martenot creates Music that smiles across the world! And the ondes Martenot creates So many tornadoes flying across the room!

And then the trumpet Blares forth with Waves of hooliganism... But the clarinet sings a Comedy show with laughter for everybody. And the flute interrupts the clarinet with a Dance around the Midnights of all the tomorrows. And the trumpet interrupts the flute with a collage of Violence. And then the timpani drums start World War III over & over again...

And that's when the chimes start to Create a mistake Growing & growing in your tummy for nine months. And the marimba starts to Send warm tropical air to Alaska & Antarctica. And the conga drums start to Play some Africa in outer space...

And the music starts to sound like a tropical festival with lots of Crazy women! The music sounds like a fun party of wife swapping! The music sounds like a joyous War! The music is a rhythmic Mathematical equation tingling your private parts! So much rhythm doing so much Heaven...

And the castanets create a Man lost in another man's wet dream. And the Maracas create some Dancing Words of graffiti art on a wall of Hysteria. And then the trumpet blares Out a shout from a human race sinking into a blood red ocean... And a trombone Masturbates some cubism together. And the French horn sounds out a Big respectable sneer. And then the tuba ruins everything with a Big explosion of natural gas...

That's when the ondes Martenot begins flying around the room again. The ondes Martenot is flying around with so much Big green monster that everybody Dives into the Big giant Pussy of the goddess in the sky! So much siLLy-siLLy-siLLy coming from that ondes Martenot! The ondes Martenot creating so much rolling Caribbean Sea...

And then all is silence...

And the female voice starts singing in Thousands of different colors. She's singing with so much Late dark night. Her voice begins creating a Series of monsters, as she sings: "I want to tell you that All the testicles in the sky Love you with so much warm gooey! And you must never tell anyone How delicious boogers can be! It will be our little secret of Monsters that Eat little children!"

And then the male voice sings: "The bullets sang to me with so much Harmony! The tornadoes were singing my name all night! I have a Tornado in my butt, would you like to pull it out?"

And then the entire chorus sings: "He has a Tornado in his butt! And she has 10,000 vibrators Creating classical music inside of her Cave of immeasurable pleasure! And everybody is having a vacation with Lots & lots of Looney tunes!"

And each voice in the chorus is a different Armageddon going on. And each different voice is creating so many different Armageddons. The chorus is a sea going in a thousand different directions...

And then the ondes Martenot starts flying about again, creating a spooky Armageddon that tastes like Hundreds of human bodies in your mouth! The musical sound is such a spooky

Sweetness, that the audience vomits beautiful things all over each other! Everything Is defecating into your ears with so much spookiness!

And the harp goes fishing for a Sweet land of Everything on fire. But the Timpani drums Interrupts the harp with Cities falling down everywhere. And the trumpet Starts creating New cities made out of musical notes. And then the Violins jump into action with a bunch of Fistfights. And the double basses cut through the violins with lots of Beautiful sunny day. And then the entire brass section jumps up and does a bunch of Dead people crawling out of the ground...

And then the piano jumps in with a Bunch of anarchy! The piano runs around with a bunch of Sadomasochistic Musical notes floating everywhere. The piano

Creates one sadomasochistic wife-swapping orgy after another. The piano has a breakfast of all the classical musical styles that came before and then shits them all at the audience. The piano plays an orgy of all the space aliens in the universe smoking crack-cocaine together.

And then the solo violin plays a chess game of crack-cocaine with another violin. And the piano plays so much crack-cocaine that the music is flying in thousands of different directions. And the solo violin then falls into a Spiraling dark well of heroin. And the piano is parachuting out of the writer's mind and into the reader's mind...

And then the harp Begins playing the writer farting. And the piano Plays a psycho artist slashing Craziness across a canvas. And the harp discovers a calm still ocean of heroin. And the piano does somersaults across the reader's consciousness...

And then the flute discovers a new world of meth-amphetamines banging on everything. And the piano Dances his way into the Virgin Mary's bedroom. And the flute Is a vibrator making the Virgin Mary so happy so very very happy. And the piano plays so many orgasms that the universe is absolutely dripping in cum...

And then the piano rushes forth into The Land of the Psychos. And the piano races around like a Ham sandwich on 10,000 legs. And the musical notes of the piano jump around the auditorium like an anal sex convention of kangaroos. And the musical notes of the piano fly around the world like Psychotic spaghetti.

And then the ondes Martenot flies around like a thousand bats flying away from a poem that's trying to eat them. And the piano's music flies around like rainbows of heroin & rainbows of crack-cocaine. And the ondes Martenot does a Voyage across a thousand centuries into a dark attic filled with the remains of the human race. And the piano does a voyage to French Impressionism...

And then as the piano forages for New worlds to create Blissful diseases in, the female singer sings: "My Pussy is On fire, and I need the entire fire department to satisfy me, I mean save me! My Pussy is So much on fire that All of Los Angeles is burning down! My Pussy is so much Desire that even the space aliens can hear my horniness from across the galaxy!"

And the piano & the female voice together sound like All the world's wild animals getting drunk together. Together, they sound like subway trains to The Virgin Mary's Vagina. They sound like all the devils of hell are invading our minds...

And as the mice in the attic in your brains start dancing To the piano, the male singer sings: "I am dying from so much Poetry! I was born with so much Blue sky in me! What Collage-of-earthquakes my life?"

And the piano & the male voice together sound like Your mother giving birth to you. Together, they sound like Two gorgeous handsome men passionately kissing each other. They sound like a thousand happy baby turtles crawling off to the sea...

And then the piano dives into a Nightmare. And the piano rises up into a Dream. And the piano runs back-&-forth like Trains going back-& forth to the reader's mind.

And the piano sounds like Hell growing out of the soil. And the piano sounds like Heaven growing out of your crotch. And the piano sounds like a bunch of ghosts in your attic playing an orchestra of the other world...

And then the oboe does some dark Gothic things with the Queen of England's Pussy. And then the oboe creates so much Penis in the medieval ages that Everybody's Pussy gets wet. And the flute jumps in and does so much cocaine with God, that God is riding the

flute to Hell. And the clarinet plays some
Comedian laughing & laughing in your
brains. And the clarinet creates a mood
of Gothic dreams & nightmares all
Entangled around you wherever you go...

And the ondes Martenot flies in with a
Rescue of endless helicopters flying in
With lots of giant dildos. The ondes
Martenot flies around like So many
demons. And the music is flying around
with so much Viruses that the entire
audience dies...

And the violins are doing so much
Nostalgia. And the violins are joined by
the cellos, and the cellos are doing so
much Fantasies up the nose. And the
violins & cellos are joined by the double
basses, and the double basses are doing
so much tickling & tickling & tickling of
the audience...

And the ondes Martenot starts creating one of your sexual fantasies. The ondes Martenot is creating so much Pornography. So much Pornography flying around in a musical chemistry that's boiling in between everybody's legs!

And all is silence...

And the flute starts to discover other universes. And the oboe is already playing in some other universe. And the clarinet is Jumping from one continent to another here on Earth. And then the saxophone jumps in with a bunch of fish jumping into the music...

And then the bassoon does some kind of Crashing of two solar systems together. And the trumpet shouts out a Crazy speech from a crazy nymphomaniac. And the trombone is creating a bunch of

Nipples floating in the air. And then the French horn Announces that dinner is ready...

And the ondes Martenot starts creating dozens of moons circling the Earth. The ondes Martenot is smashing up against the shores of all the planets out there. The ondes Martenot is releasing thousands of balloons of Crazy faces into the upper reaches of your mind...

And the entire chorus sings: "Our voices are acrobats jumping & flying & floating through all the daydreams of the reader! Our emotions are flying off to everything impossible and back again! Our heresies are Celebrated throughout the Land of Happy Endings! Our sexual genitalia are Conquering literature & painting & sculpture & architecture with so much Pornography! We must Paint lots of pornography with our voices! And we must Go to hell where we will be deliriously happy now!"

And the voices of the chorus sound like so much Tarantulas walking around the ceiling & walls & floors of the auditorium. The voices sound like Snakes slithering all over the ceiling & walls & floors. Their singing voices sound like Hundreds of noisy jackhammers making love to each other...

And then the male singer sings: "So much cancer growing in our heads! So many solar systems flying around in our testicles! So much volcanoes & more volcanoes & more volcanoes to feel!"

And the violins do a Vacation to all the nooks & crannies of your mind. And the cellos do a Stampede of masculine lust across the City. And the double basses do some crab fishing in the Bering Sea...

And then the piano rushes forth into a Frenzy of Nostalgia. The piano rushes around like a giant monster with a knife chasing the conductor around & around the auditorium. The piano is a rushing Steamroller crushing puritanism into the dust...

And the ondes Martenot rushes around like Strawberries with legs running around the music. The ondes Martenot rushes forth like Blueberries with wings flying around your head. The ondes Martenot rushing around & around like Automobiles that can't find a planet...

And then the entire symphony orchestra together starts playing The Garden of Cock Sucking. Every instrument is playing the reader's cock being sucked.

Everything sounds like cock sucking & more cock sucking & more cock sucking. It sounds like so much art being created with jizz...

And then the female singer sings: "My voice comes to you with so much Yearning for Bright colors like blue & green & orange! The words I sing reach you with so much Greasy greasy Happy! My voice is a Journey across a desert of Feelings!"

And the male singer sings: "When your voice sings to me I Can't believe my Penis! When your words reach my ears I Want to jump off a tall building! Your voice means so much Brightly-colored polka dots to me!"

And now the harp is playing all the ghosts of a closed factory building. And then the entire orchestra plays an ethnic genocide together. And then the harp plays lots of fairytales with stabbing knives. And that's when the entire orchestra responds with lots of comets & asteroids crashing into the planet Earth. And now the harp is playing lots of naked women walking around the auditorium. And the entire orchestra answers with lots of big Hungry dinosaurs flying out of their instruments...

And the piano plays a cOnStaNtLy-cHaNgiNg-cUbiSt-pOrtRaiT. And the orchestra responds by playing a bunch of cartoon characters having a cannibalistic banquet. And the piano responds to the orchestra by playing lots of Human meat hanging from the ceiling of the public market. And that's when the orchestra responds to the piano by playing lots of Avant-garde composers vomiting Poetry in lots of bright colors all over the audience. And then the piano & the orchestra start fighting each other. The piano is playing Walt Whitman getting fucked up the ass by a very horny Tyrannosaurus Rex, while the orchestra is playing lots of toilets, and the ondes Martenot is playing merry-go-rounds of Hysteria devouring everyone's brains...

And then there's silence...

And the solo violin starts playing a big bus crashing into the music. And the orchestra answers with lots of big buses crashing into the stars. And the solo violin answers with lots of clouds in the sky. And the orchestra answers with Everybody on the planet Earth having a nervous breakdown. And the solo violin answers with a kiss. And the orchestra answers with thousands of bears eating all the English literature that's ever been written...

And the flute starts playing some Fantastic Big boogers flying all over the world. And so the orchestra starts playing some Fantastic Big buttocks shaking & shaking Like fleshy earthquakes. And the flute is now playing Everything delicious. And the orchestra responds by playing a big loud Delicious. And now the flute is playing a gentle bullet Flying through the air at midnight. And the orchestra answers the flute with lots of Artillery that's Blasting the status quo into pieces...

And then the trumpet plays lots of transsexual spiders crawling everywhere. And so the orchestra plays lots of transsexual space aliens riding a ferris wheel into a most beautiful oblivion. And the trumpet begins playing Howling monkeys searching for clues to the origin of the universe. And the orchestra shouts out a big loud Disease. And the trumpet is creating So many diseases. And the orchestra answers the trumpet with lots of Siamese cats crawling everywhere...

And now the female singer is singing: "So many diseases that feel like Hungry children devouring all the stars in the sky! We love these diseases that Eat holes through the universe! I want to have sex with all the Mysterious men walking into my bedroom!"

And now the entire symphony orchestra answers with lots of flying pigs flying around the auditorium. The entire symphony orchestra is playing so much Flying pigs. The entire orchestra is creating a bunch of Noises of wild animals fucking together...

And now the male singer is singing: "I love flying pigs because They feel good in my Vagina! And I love all the beautiful philosophical words of flying pigs, because My bellybutton is swallowing up the universe! What do we do with all the Sexy giraffes in miniskirts waiting for clients on the street corners?"

And the entire symphony orchestra answers with so Many solar systems being Eaten by your nightmares. The entire symphony orchestra is playing lots of Nightmares. The symphony orchestra sounds like a bunch of inanimate objects in the attic all fornicating with each other...

And now the entire chorus is singing: "The nightmares that Create new ugly worlds! We are blessed with nightmares that Swallow us with a giant Gothic mouth! We are blessed With boogers in our Political speeches and boogers in our Civic duties and boogers in our Pledge of Allegiance!"

And the symphony orchestra starts playing Your body splintering up into thousands of different directions. The symphony Orchestra is playing lots of Loving confusion together. All the instruments are racing forth in a frenzy of Extinct animals all dancing together across the Floors of art museums across the world...

And the violins strive for the next horizon filled with Herpes sores! And the violins rise up into a giant tidal wave of herpes! And the violins rise & rise all the way up to Heaven!

And the cellos strive to achieve the perfect bellybutton! And the cellos try to Jump up the hills of Verbs. Meanwhile, nouns Are drooling everywhere All over the music! And the cellos are achieving So much herpes That God's Penis in heaven erupts with a Beautiful collage of herpes sores!

And the double basses jump in and try to Dominate the show with lots of Erotic storms of flying nipples! And the double basses are trying to Reinvent the universe! And the double basses are trying to recreate new childhoods for everybody!

And the piano rises forth! And the piano is trying to Become thousands of things in this single moment! And the piano player is trying to be thousands of monsters creating music! And the piano

is trying to Make summer come back
again, but winter keeps on Knocking on
your door!

And faster & faster goes the piano into
All the paradise of hell! And faster &
faster the piano tries to Climb over every
impossible mountain in his way! And with
a faster & faster Psychosis the piano
keys start inventing new monsters every
second!

And the bassoon throws in a Dark Gothic
fairytale. And the flute throws in some
Delicious scrambled eggs. And the
trumpet creates a Feast of everything
barbaric & monstrous. And the trombone
is Creating so many Aztec princesses
that The streets are exploding with sexy!

And the male singer sings: "Everything
barbaric & monstrous is so much Dark
forest growing in my brains! So much

Musical notes crashing into the inside walls of my head! And that's why we celebrate Drive-by shootings with lots of champagne!"

And the female singer sings: "Celebrate the Sky becoming crooked with lAugHinG-cOrrUpt-hYeNaS buying their way into heaven! Celebrate the little children crawling out of Our genitals and becoming adults tomorrow morning! Celebrate the Seas of pornography that drown us with Lust!"

And the ondes Martenot starts doing So much surrealistic impossibilities that everything disappears. The ondes Martenot becomes zillions of flying snakes flying through the sky. The ondes Martenot starts weaving together a graffiti mural. The ondes Martenot begins searching every nook & cranny of everybody's brains...

And all is the wild & crazy of Your imagination Marching off into so many wild blue yonders. The music sounds like Your imagination has become Kidnapped by some Goat in the Himalayas. The music is so much Outhouse overflowing with the imaginations of a thousand artists....

And then the flute softly settles into a Century of Everywhere tiptoeing back & forth. And the harp gently taps the reader on the shoulder. And with delicacy the flute Whispers of your death into the reader's Ear...

But the timpani drums Begin shaking everything in the universe. And the timpani drums are Crashing all of history into pieces. And the timpani drums are

Rediscovering the orgasms of the great giants of the clouds...

And then the solo violin plays a lovely Walk through a prison full of inmates...

But the timpani drums interrupt with a loud bout of sunshine...

And the flute creates a heaven of Sadomasochism in all the dungeons of the world...

But the timpani drums interrupt again with so much Heavenly blow jobs & Pussy eating that everybody in the audience has an orgasm!

And the harp does a sweet Doughnut in your mouth...

But then the clarinet mocks the harp with Lots of laughing monsters...

And the trumpet shouts down the clarinet with so much red & blue & green!

And the solo violin goes on a pleasant Killing spree...

But the tuba interrupts with a Smelly comment on the meaning of life!

And then the chorus sings together: "It smells like Wild animals getting lost inside your head! It smells like Oceans of Words splashing around your brains! Everything smells like the reader's thoughts becoming a symphony that drifts outwards into a musical fantasy that fills the universe!"

And the solo violin plays so much winter. The solo violin plays so much darkness. The solo violin plays a world with so little hope...

But then the clarinet lightens everything up with a Summer breeze. And the clarinet tells us of Endless menstrual fluids flowing down the walls of the auditorium... And the trumpet jumps in with a laugh. And the tuba Laughs as well. But the harp is crying...

And the flute tries to comfort the harp with a touch of Cold death. But the trombone Crashes into the flute with a Happy party tune. And the solo violin rushes around the trombone with a Quick sprint of Joy...

And the chorus sings together: "Rush around with lots of Yeast infections! Rush-rush-rush everywhere with so much Sexually-transmitted diseases to generously share with everyone! Always rushing to The booty world of Now, And rushing to The Land of Whispers where Wishes grow like weeds!"

And then the entire symphony orchestra together plays an Ottoman palace filled with luxurious sensuous sin. And the orchestra plays The entire world on fire. And the orchestra plays Autumn kissing springtime with so much Bullets that everyone goes dancing to the graveyard. And as the orchestra plays, a hoard of Russian folk dancers jump & dance onto the stage...

And the orchestra plays the human race sinking into a Dark dungeon, While the Russian folk dancers dance like Happy & sad making love all afternoon. And as the orchestra plays Millions of years of sunshine, the Russian folk dancers dance Around the world on fire. And as the orchestra plays So much space alien food, the Russian folk dancers dance Lots of erotic space alien stuff...

And suddenly the orchestra stops. And the Russian folk dancers stop dancing and freeze...

And the male singer sings: "Space alien food tastes like a journey into a factory of Cat meows! Space alien food is as delicious as Pornographic poetry! Give me that space alien food!"

And the female singer sings: "Millions of years of sunshine on my naked body! Everything Screams with millions of years of sunshine! So much sunshine that Your desires & emotions are Bigger than the sky!"

And suddenly the orchestra starts playing again. And the Russian dancers start dancing again. And the orchestra is playing All the great artists of history jizzy-ing all over each other, and the Russian dancers are dancing a dance welcoming the audience to a nuclear war. And the orchestra is playing a tunnel of Love with lots of Diseases calling your name, and the Russian dancers are dancing 60 billion galaxies all Jumping in front of you...

And suddenly the music stops. And the Russian dancers stop dancing and freeze.

And the flute starts to play a Russian roulette love song. And the cello does a Giant ravine filled with dead human bodies all saying hello. And the piano does a tWisStiNg-tuRniNg-aLLeYwaY with lots of Tomato sauce...

And then the entire orchestra jumps to life, and starts to play The reader going insane... And the Russian folk dancers jump to life, and start to Dance their way all the way to The reader's house. And the orchestra is playing the Amazon rainforest burning down. And the Russian dancers are dancing All the planets suddenly falling to pieces. And the orchestra is playing Too many strawberries. And the Russian dancers are dancing aBsTraCt-eXpResSioNisT-jiZz splattered all over the Mona Lisa in the Louvre...

And then the orchestra is silent. The Russian dancers freeze in place.

And the piano starts to play a Man eating his own brains. And the harp joins in with lots & Lots of female orgasms flowing down the walls of the auditorium... And the solo violin creates a mural of All your emotions devouring everything.

And then the entire chorus sings: "The female orgasm! A Triumph of gargoyles with giant tongues that feel in your Pussy like jackhammers of joy! Lots of female orgasms with The Mushroom clouds! Endless endless female orgasms with so much Joy!"

And then the orchestra jumps to life, and starts to play Insane space aliens dancing on the planet Earth. And the Russian dancers jump to life, and start imitating so many different species of space aliens dancing for all eternity... And the orchestra plays All of your dead ancestors dancing around you, and the Russian dancers dance Lots of 14th century art rioting into the 21st century...

And then, as the orchestra plays an eternal midnight, the Russian dancers dance off the stage...

And then the male singer sings: "When I eat my own body it tastes like Andy Warhol giving head to Genghis Khan!"

And the female singer sings: "My body tastes like World War One!"

And then the entire chorus sings: "Our bodies taste like all the fires of hell! Does the audience want to eat us?"

And then suddenly each violin plays a different yesterday, and a totally different tomorrow. And each cello plays a different Stroll through the insane asylum. And each double bass plays a group of space aliens chasing World War III down the street...

Meanwhile, the flute is Playing all the clouds floating off the planet Earth and into one of your dreams. And meanwhile, the vibes are creating Your sexy wife walking down the street to a hotel where she will meet a stranger. And the clarinet starts playing Circus animals rampaging all over Heaven...

And then, all the woodwinds start playing a chaotic Game of chess with each other. And the entire brass section starts playing a Smiling kind of chaos. And all the strings are playing so much chaos...

And then the piano descends into a violent chaos, and the timpani drums answer the piano with lots of Civilizations bursting open. And the tuba blurts out an Obscenity. And the bassoon blurts out a Foggy morning full of mystery. And then the triangle starts playing All the wild wild characters of the wild wild American West invading a children's cartoon show...

And the whole time, the violin players are plucking their violins with the rhythms of hunger. And the rhythm is like taking your clothes off on a freezing day in Antarctica. And the rhythm is like Everybody on the planet Earth playing Russian roulette with each other...

And then the entire chorus sings: "We want to freeze to death on a Happy day! We want to burn under the hot sun! We want So many tornadoes in our private parts!"

And then the entire orchestra starts to play country-western madness. It's a country-western madness of Schoenberg & a cowboy having anal sex On a space satellite revolving & revolving around the planet Earth... It's a country western madness of Gothic monsters from the 13th century line-dancing through the Wild-wild-West...

And that's when the country-western dancers come jumping & dancing out onto the stage. And as the country-western dancers dance like rocket ships to one of the reader's fantasies, the orchestra plays so much country-western bLow jobs. And the dancers are dancing so much country-western outer space with lots of Egyptian Hieroglyphics thrown in. And so much country-western Sunny afternoons in Japan are being created by the orchestra...

And your ears are Relishing all this musical sunlight. And your eyes are Filled with musical notes flying through the air. And together, your eyes & ears are Walking across a thousand different places you've never been to before, your eyes and ears are Swimming across a Very naughty universe, and your eyes and ears are Drowning in so many sounds & imagery that You jump into a big black hole and never come back...

And as the orchestra plays country-western madness, and as all the dancers dance country-western madness, the chorus starts to sing...

The chorus sings: "We swim through the madness of This moment! Our voices are journeys of madness into Dark childhoods Storming into our adult lives! Our voices are Made out of knives!"

And the orchestra continues playing a slaughterhouse of human beings on a pleasant summer day. And the country-western dancers continue dancing amongst decapitated human heads floating in the air. And the music sounds like gunshots & painting & an orgy. And the dancing all looks like cracks of upcoming disaster appearing all over the world...

And the orchestra plays All the buildings near & far falling down. And the country-western dancers dance to the stars in the sky exploding all over the audience. And the entire audience Is having a nineteenth century opium hallucination. That's when the male singer begins to sing...

He sings: "Look at my Ulcerous skin Laughing with So much Other-worldly beings feasting on my skin!"

And the female singer sings: "Why? Is your Spaceship not cumming with lots of Rabies?"

And the chorus sings: "Your decapitated head is in the mail!"

And then the orchestra plays a Determined man digging his way all the way to hell. And the country-western dancers start to dance off the stage...

And now the orchestra starts to play a different Delicious piece of pie. The orchestra starts playing a different Boiling vat of hallucinations... It's a completely different Circus full of All the characters from your childhood all stabbing each other to death!

And then the timpani drums smash everything into pieces with a Smile! And the tuba goes wild with some Pornography! And the piano throws in a Description of a beautiful naked lady. And the flute does some Beastiality, while a cello does some Cocaine with a rhinoceros playing the harp, and the chimes suddenly start Doing somersaulting hurricanes all over the place...

And the male singer sings: "So much cocaine with all the meowing cats in the garden!"

And the female singer sings: "Too much cocaine with all the space aliens!"

And the chorus sings: "Lots of cocaine with all the cavemen from prehistory!"

And then the orchestra jumps forth into a Hallucinatory trip of all of Babylon falling out of your butthole! The orchestra starts playing lots of Hallucinations! So much Hallucinations the orchestra is creating! All the sounds entering your ears are so much Outer space!

And that's when a bunch of ballet dancers start dancing onto the stage.

And as the music plays, the ballet dancers create the taste of delicious lollipops with their bodies, the ballet dancers dance like Volcanoes in spring, they dance like so much Herpes that you've never been so ecstatically happy in your life...

And then the symphony orchestra falls silent. And the flute starts playing a waltz with Lots of dancing beavers. And the ballet dancers dance to the flute. The ballet dancers dance like Waltzes of Crazy testicles on fire. They dance like Waltzes of Wild animals Waltzing on a tightrope from Paris to a giant space alien's nipple. They dance like Lots of chickens jumping through the windows of This book...

And the flute is playing so much insane gobbledygook as the ballet dancers dance. The flute is playing lots of Teenagers losing their virginity. The flute plays So many space alien invaders having sex with everybody's wives that Everybody's mothers has an orgasm...

And as the flute plays, and as the ballet dancers dance, the male singer sings...

The male singer sings: "Sticking your Penis into a world war is the answer! Saturn's rings going around & around Your insanity! It's the answer to all the little Words eating through our guts! It's the answer to Being swallowed by the toilet for all eternity!"

And the flute plays more Teenagers losing their virginity in the Orgies of Cartoon characters on your television set. And the ballet dancers dance more Spaceships arriving on the planet Earth, as the female singer sings...

She sings: "Praise the Flying elephants in sexy lingerie! Praise the Planets revolving around the Big Penis! Praise the Penises that move like pistons in-&-out of these poems!"

And then the entire chorus sings together as the ballet dancers dance...

The chorus sings: "So much Turbulent jizz seas to navigate! So many Zigzagging poetry phrases for all the blank walls demanding to be painted on! How do we Rebuild the crazy-crazy into something even crazier?"

And then all the instruments in the orchestra jump up and begin playing a bunch of Four letter words – they're playing So much lust – They're playing beautiful sculptures of beautiful men & women doing beautiful things. And the ballet dancers are dancing Nuclear missiles flying from Russia towards the USA, they're dancing World War III with so much love, and they're dancing With lots of decapitated heads that are laughing & laughing...

And then the piano plays a romantic encounter with all the sheep floating in outer space, and the ballet dancers dance all the mathematical equations in a young mathematician's brains...

And then the clarinet plays a drive-by shooting with lots of laughter & love, and the ballet dancers dance all the holes in your brains...

And then the harp plays some Vaginas full of nuclear missiles, and the ballet dancers dance some Sweet heart attacks with Lots of yummy dark chocolate...

And then the entire orchestra jumps forth into a Percy B. Shelley poem with lots of Daggers, and the ballet dancers dance off the stage. And as the ballet dancers dance off the stage, they dance like Verbs going to a cocaine convention, they dance like Nouns going to the insane asylum, and they dance like Adjectives going to Bed with you...

And now the solo violin plays a Mischievous grin. And the piano plays city streets full of Magical words. And the trumpet plays a massive insane get together of all the massively insane people of the massively insane world...

And the male singer sings: "It's a city of Unusual personalities On fire! It's a city of Love with so much Hate! It's a city of words that keeps boiling over with more words & more words & more words!"

And the chimes start to do so much church services with Pussy juices, and

the triangle is Calling everyone to eat
Pussy, and the vibes are Musically eating
Giant parts of everyone's brains...

And that's when the female singer sings:
"I love to eat Pussy with So much
musical tongue! I love to eat Pussy with
escargot! Pussy is so much Wild frontiers
of Penis running & running around for
years in a circle!"

And the violin starts to play so much
nostalgia & longing & loneliness... The
violin is playing a lot of Happy times in
an old person's past... The violin is
playing a thousand madmen standing in
line to eat your wife's Pussy...

And then the entire symphony Orchestra
jumps alive and starts creating Lots of
fantasies flooding through the
auditorium. The orchestra creates So
many bellybuttons swallowing the

audience. The orchestra creates a giant Pussy Eating Holiday celebrated throughout the world...

And as the orchestra creates a new world, the modern dancers start to dance their way onto the stage... And as the orchestra plays Your life Jumping all around you, the modern dancers dance so much nipple happiness, they dance so much Disease, They dance so many similes & metaphors, that all the world's elephants want to eat your Pussy with their huge trunks, the modern dancers dance like a lot of Words having a nervous breakdown together...

And then the orchestra falls silent. The flute plays so much Flatulence, and the modern dancers move like Whales swimming across So many mysteries. And then the piccolo plays a lot of

Crunchy-crunchy-Crunchy, and the modern dancers move with So much Perverted logic. And the piano starts to create so much Summertime, and the modern dancers create so much Summertime with the movements of their bodies...

And the entire symphony orchestra starts playing Your brains Burning with lots of ideas, and the modern dancers start dancing Your brains Flying around in loops & Circles & somersaults. And all the instruments in the orchestra are creating a mental asylum together, and all the modern dancers are creating iNsAnE-dAnCiNg-mAniFesToeS together. And the music of the orchestra is going to the moon & back. And the modern dancers are dancing to the moon & back...

And the symphony orchestra falls silent...

And the harp plays like Swiss cheese & ham, and the modern dancers dance like Swiss cheese & ham...

And the piano plays like Your mother having fun with the vibrator, and the modern dancers dance like viBraToRs & vIbRatOrS & viBrAtoRs...

And the piccolo plays like a mouse swallowing the entire English language, and the modern dancers dance like the English language going insane...

And then the male singer sings a bunch of funny made-up words, And the modern dancers dance a bunch of funny made-up words together...

And then the female singer sings a lot of Bawdy jokes, and the modern dancers dance a lot of bad & bawdy & bad & bawdy & bad & bawdy...

And then the chorus sings softly a bunch of Rats devouring each other, and the modern dancers dance a bunch of Rats scurrying everywhere...

And then the entire orchestra comes to life. And the orchestra is playing the world's biggest loudest whorehouse, and the modern dancers are dancing the dance of prostitutes & clients & pimps & madams. And the orchestra is playing poison roses growing all over the auditorium, and the modern dancers are dancing like poison roses growing everywhere. And the orchestra is playing war & more war & more war, and the modern dancers are dancing war & more war & more war...

And as the orchestra plays, body parts are falling off of everybody. And the modern dancers start dancing off the stage...

And then the orchestra really comes to life with a bunch of suns & moons & planets crashing into each other! And the orchestra is racing forward with so much thrust & speed & power! And the orchestra is racing forward & forward with velocity & veloooooooooooocity & velocityyyyyyyyyyyy! All the instruments are playing a fast fast fast!

And the rhythm is like all the world's wild animals chasing after each other! And the rhythm is like Siamese twins hacking each other into pieces! It's such a fast fast rhythm gushing everywhere! So much fast fast rhythm that's Punching the audience in the face!

And the violins & cellos & double basses are fast fast Animals flying everywhere! The strings are Crack-cocaine volcanoes erupting Sexually transmitted diseases everywhere! It's so much fast fast Crazy that all the dead composers in cemeteries around the world jump out of their graves and start dancing! And the strings are throwing rhythms on top of rhythms on top of more rhythms! So many rhythms built on top of other rhythms! So many different wild rhythms going South to Pluto and then north to Jupiter and then east to the sun and West to the moon!

And the woodwinds are all creating so much Giant circus balloons floating everywhere! The woodwinds are throwing into the air so much wiLd-aNiMaL-fEeLinG! Lots of Wild four-letter words flying from the woodwinds!

And the brass section is throbbing with powerful Emotions! And the brass section is all blurting out so much Shocking news! The brass section is creating so much Hurricanes inside of each & every one of us! Each instrument in the brass section igniting the Universe with so much Musical fire!

And the vibes are doing so much Sex! The vibes are going all crazy directions! The vibes are creating so much Sex so fast! Fast fast fast the vibes are Making all the men's Penises in the audience rise & rise!

And then the timpani drums start doing so many volcanoes! The timpani drums turn all the oceans into Stormy-emotional-convulsions of Now! The timpani drums going so Berserk with musical nipples raining down on the

human race! The timpani drums
Drumming & Drumming with so much
violence and more violence and more
violence!

And the violins are suddenly seized with
violence! It's a fast fast violence as the
violins are searching for other planets –
searching for other musical languages to
create – searching for other sexual
revolutions to set musical scores to!
Trembling forth with so much rebellion
smashing through tyranny the violins are
the voices of the voiceless!

And the cellos are infected with the
violence as well! The cellos are born with
violence! The violence erupting so fast
and so quickly from cellos going so right
& left at the same time! The cellos are
Marching from one planet to another!

And the double basses are flying dragons
flying so quickly quickly! Flying so
quickly through all the musical circus the
double basses! The double basses are
erupting over & over again with so much
Wild luscious fruit growing out of the
music!

And all the woodwinds are possessed
with a thousand spirits of the Devil! The
woodwinds all possessed with so much
Devil as they play so much Happy & Sin
dancing together! The woodwinds are all
Discovering new Continents floating
around the planet Earth! Everything is of
fast angry chaos as the woodwinds do so
much sunrises & sunsets flying through
the centuries!

And the brass section throws out so
much castrated Penis into the music! The
music infected with so much MeNtaL-

hEaLth-pRobLemS! The brass section throwing so much passion into the music! Each musical note flying forth from the brass section is a Knife-stabbing glory of passion! Passion and more passion and more passion Jumping from the music!

And that's when the ondes Martenot begins its Journey through all the communities of madness inside your head! The bizarre musical notes of the ondes Martenot flying through the music like Comets made of methamphetamine crashing into the Earth! The ondes Martenot flying its musical notes across the solar system – across the universe – across the everything! The ondes Martenot creating so much Flying everything!

And then all is silence...

And the male singer sings: "So much methamphetamine to sing! A fast-fast motorcycle ride through this musical universe being created by the composer! So much wonderful hell surrounding you, as you drive through musical notes crashing down the highway!"

And the female singer sings: "Her Pussy tastes like Musical rioting spontaneously Rupturing in all the streets of the world! Her Pussy juices are so delicious that Mozart jumps out of his grave to create Lots of new musical nipples! Her Pussy juices create so much dAnCiNg-aLbeRt-eiNsTeiN-mUsiC that You can't stop dancing to her Pussy juices!"

And the chorus sings: "Fuck that Pussy with a paintbrush given to you by Picasso! Eat that Pussy with so much

You! Eat that Pussy until You lose your tongue forever!"

And all is once again silence...

And the solo violin begins plucking away at its strings, and drops of paint, drops of color, are created by the plucking violin...

And then all the violins begin plucking away at their strings, and all the plucking of the violins is creating drops of paint falling everywhere throughout the auditorium, drops of color falling everywhere...

And then the solo cello begins creating a dark painting. The solo cello paints a canvas of Human suffering dripping everywhere... The solo cello paints So many Dostoyevsky personalities entering & leaving the subway train car. And the solo cello paints a universe of human

personalities all drooling all over each
other...

And then all the cellos begin painting
together. Together, all the cellos paint So
much lust Fermenting & Lurking &
Stalking throughout the city, and the
cellos paint So many images that itch
with that Unstoppable glow of human
desire, and they paint So much Paul
Gauguin that all the northern cities are
dripping with florescent tropical colors...

And then the piano begins painting a
gruesome scene of Misery drowning the
entire city in poverty & homelessness &
desperation. It's a scene of Dark colors
being painted by the piano. It's a scene
of So many Santa Claus clones climbing
up into the anus of Satan. It's a scene of
Winter that never ends with its big
masochism swallowing your soul...

And the piccolo joins the scene being painted by the piano. And the piccolo is adding Joyous Youth to the scene. The Flute is adding a sexy tornado of Adolescent hormones fermenting & fermenting as high school lets out. And the piccolo is adding a drawing of a nude sketched with the dark colors of the night...

And that's when the trumpet gushes out a huge invasion filled with universes of color! And all the instruments in the brass section suddenly start gushing out all kinds of light & dark colors everywhere. The entire brass section is exploding with color! All the colors flooding out of the brass section are having sex with the world!

And then the timpani drums start creating revolutions of color, and wars of color, and earthquakes of color! And the timpani drums start smashing the old art movements into pieces, and creating new art movements! The timpani drums keep creating one revolution in art after another! The timpani drums are destroying & rebuilding & destroying & rebuilding! And the timpani drums are pounding with all the desperate wretches of the human race pounding & pounding on the doors of the rich with a cannibalistic hunger!

And then all is silence...

And the harp starts to softly create her own painting. And the painting the harp is creating is Licking the reader with color! And the harp is creating an afternoon orgy of Art Nouveau! And the harp is creating a Forever dream of symbolism. And the harp is creating the sensual world where all your erotic dreams come true...

And then the solo violin becomes a paintbrush painting the awakening of puberty in all the young ones. And the solo violin is painting thrusting titties Growing out of the young ladies chests with its paintbrush. The paintbrush of the solo violin is a Creator of sin, the paintbrush of the solo violin is a Creator of stories, and the paintbrush of the solo violin is creating so much Color that everybody in the audience drowns in its brightness...

And then the trombone throws an onslaught of images into the air! The images that the trombone creates are made out of the reader's dreams. And the trombone is creating a river of images that Surround the reader in the eternity after death. The trombone is creating the readers' ghost dancing in the graveyard for eternity...

And then the French horn creates a Romantic era painting filled with so much giant movement. And then the French horn creates a Baroque painting filled with sins of joy. And then the French horn creates a mural that lives & breeds with so much You!

And then the ondes Martenot starts throwing rivers of images everywhere! And the ondes Martenot starts creating seas of bright colors Coming to life! The ondes Martenot starts creating waves of words in bright colors that splash & splash throughout the auditorium...

And then the vibes begin creating one Matisse after another... The vibes are creating a room full of Matisse canvases... The vibes are creating a beautiful sensual Eternity where the reader can Live in a fantasy world forever...

And then the solo violin begins weaving together a Cubist painting. The thrashing lines of the painting are created by the slashing thrusts of the solo violin. The solo violin creating so much agitation & thunder & seething feelings. The solo violin creating and creating and creating...

And then a cello & a double bass start to create so much Vincent van Gogh together... The cello & the double bass creating so many paintings of Vincent van Gogh... The cello & the double bass seethe with so much van Gogh...

And then the harp begins creating a Paul Gauguin painting. The harp is singing with so much color! The harp is Crying with so much color! The colors created from the harp are Sweet and Soft and Cuddly...

Then the timpani drums begin creating explosions of color! So much color exploding everywhere! So many images flying everywhere, as the timpani drums boom & boom & boom...

And then the male singer starts to sing a painting: "When I paint my painting I paint So many of my faces floating around a Graveyard! I paint so many poverty-stricken wretches Screeching all around me! I paint so much raving lunacy! I paint so much Emotional volcano! I paint with so much feeling that I Feel that I could conquer all of the imaginary world with my painting!"

And then the female singer starts to sing a different painting: "My painting is full of so many Vaginas that I lick & lick in all my fantasies of Darkness! My painting is endless words filled with endless breasts & asses of all the ladies I want to love! My colors flow with the love of a woman loving another woman! My painting is so much poetry flowing out of my Vagina!"

And then the chorus starts to sing lots of paintings: "This painting in our heads is a seething volcano that never ends! We want so much Forever in this painting! We will create all the curses & blessings of humanity with this painting!"

And then the ondes Martenot begins to travel everywhere with the graffiti Art on trains traveling everywhere... And all the instruments in the orchestra join the ondes Martenot in painting so much

Graffiti art everywhere... All the instruments painting graffiti art on everything in every city on Earth...

And then the violins start playing orgies! And the rhythm is Going up & down and back & forth like a giant orgy without gravity! And the orgies are So many wives throwing themselves at strangers to procreate babies of lust! And the violins are Thrusting like penises! And the violins are trembling like female bodies on the verge of orgasms and more orgasms and more orgasms! And the violins are playing orgies and more orgies and more orgies!

And the cellos join the orgies! And the orgies are So musical! And the cellos are writhing & aaahing & oooohing with the orgies! And the rhythms are Filled with so many immaculate conceptions! So many cellos doing so much Sex and so much pleasure and so much Naughty!

And the double basses join the orgies too! And the orgies are The joys of the kingdoms of pleasure! And the music is So much pleasure dancing all around your ears! And the rhythms are Fornicating so many melodies together! And the double basses are Tickling the reader with So many happy musical notes!

And then the trumpet howls with orgies! And the trumpet is howling & howling & howling! And the trumpet is rainbows of sex And floods of lust And downpours of spermatozoa! It's so much wet Pussy juices in the musical notes!

And the piano paints a cOnStantLy-mOviNg-mUraL of orgies! So much orgies! So much piano! So much Sexual revolution bursting through the dams of Puritanism! And the piano Summons the masses to the Festivals of Sex! And the orgies are So musical that all the musicians are ejaculating musical notes into their pants! And the piano is giving the rhythm a Sexual hallelujah so happy that the reader goes insane with joy!

And then the clarinet announces even more orgies! The clarinet announces even More erect Penises for all to enjoy! The clarinet announces giant Vagina caves for all to live in!

And the piccolo does so many blow jobs! The piccolo does blow jobs & more blow jobs & more bowl jobs! The piccolo is playing so Much homoerotic joy that Butt fucking rituals in the Vatican begin at once! The piccolo is Playing balloons flying up into the Imaginations of all the birds...

And the oboe approves of the orgies with a sigh. The oboe does some Traveling across the The thoughts in your mind. The oboe does lots of Loops of Lunacy around the Looney Tunes asylum...

And then those vibes set the mood for more orgies. More orgies & more orgies & more orgies! The vibes are Breathing life into the orgies! The vibes are Sending out So many legions of colorful jellyfish floating across the air of the auditorium. The vibes sound like Cool Limp Penises that have been satisfied by hours & hours of sex & orgasms...

And then the chorus starts to moan & moan with all the orgies. The chorus starts to Belch out words & Rhythms with so much Nastiness! The voices of the chorus are So many guillotines on your Sunday afternoon. The music sounds like People screaming while they're jumping off of planets. The rhythms of the voices of the chorus are so many exotic colors surrounding you with Everything erotic...

And the harp gives an orgasmic sigh of relief. The harp sighs with so many orgasms. Orgasms & more orgasms & more orgasms!

And the timpani drums play orgasms & more orgasms & more orgasms! The timpani drums are cumming & cumming & cumming! The rhythms of the timpani drums booming & booming & booming are Creating new worlds at the edges of our imaginations!

And then the cymbals start clashing & clashing & clashing! The rhythms of the cymbals are Suicidal & Homicidal clashing over & over again! And the music is Such a delicious cake of homicide & suicide. The music is Dancing between homicide & suicide. The cymbals are Crashing together reality & unreality. And the timpani drums are Turning all the world's cities into nightmares of So much reality stalking you...

And then the chorus starts to sing: "You the audience are our Delicious baked bread! We kiss you audience with so much Winter storms! You the audience are our Salvation of endless faces bouncing all the way up to the heavens & back! And that's why Jesus Christ blesses this orgy with lots of cum!"

And then the solo violin plays the beginning of a burning flame. The solo violin plays a flame growing & growing until the entire symphony is on fire...

And then another violin joins in with a
second flame that's burning & burning.
The second violin plays a breakfast of
suicide & a lunch of murder & a dinner of
rape...

And then a third violin joins the other
two violins. And the third violin is playing
yet another burning flame. And the third
violin is playing Everyone climbing up the
staircase of eternity & Everyone walking
into a forever darkness...

And together, the three violins are
playing three different rhythms. Three
different rhythms that Spike & Dangle &
Lunge. Three different rhythms that
Thrash with love & hate & despair...

And then the solo cello joins the three
violins. And the cello adds so much
night. And the cello is alive & dead with

so much Magical forest growing all around him as he plays...

And then the double bass jumps in with its own struggles of hope & despair. And the double bass adds its own seasoning of miracles to the music. And the double bass is playing blood & more blood & more blood...

And the female singer sings: "I was a lobotomized ghost dancing by a Medieval stream of flowing-rabid-words! It was Flying saucers in my Vagina! So much Wild & crazy growing out of all the Musical notes!"

And the male singer sings: "In a jiffy I Conquered the space aliens with my poetry! It was a Sinking city of Paranoia! It was so much incest that I had to Chop off my penis!"

And the chorus sings: "So much rage & sadness & despair! So much bright sunshine to feel sadness with! So many thunderstorms of fear inside of you!"

And then the chimes try to change the mood with a Wacky Wacky Wackiness. The flute seeks to create a new day with Lots of musical notes of masturbation. And the harp tries to soothe with Soft dark colors being created by the music...

And then the timpani drums go on the warpath again with a bunch of Blasts of irony & laughter. And the trumpet plays a night of sin in hell. And the clarinet does lots of hellos...

And then the solo violin plays a naked lady posing for a painter. And the solo violin plays a river that flows through All your aches & pains. And the solo violin plays So many magical thunderstorms of wild & free, as the painter paints a music full of images...

And the flute plays a naked woman posing for a photographer. And the flute is playing with so much sensuality. And the flute is playing so much whorehouses & more whorehouses & whorehouses...

And then the piano begins to play a couple making love. And the harp joins in, and together the piano & the harp sound like two twins attacking each other with chainsaws, they sound like the planet Earth & the moon crashing & crashing into each other. And the couple makes love with the piano & harp playing sensuous Art Nouveau scenery around them...

And then the solo violin plays a woman having fun with a vibrator. And the piano joins in, and together the violin & the

piano sound like God pissing human
history out of his Penis, the violin &
piano sound like Violent madmen
Growing like Deranged flowers out of all
the music, and as the woman has fun
with her vibrator the piano & the violin
create Exciting visions all around her...

And then all the naked women & naked
men in paintings all over the world
suddenly jump out of those paintings –
and they jump on stage – and start
dancing as the entire orchestra Plays lots
of fish swimming everywhere, as the
entire orchestra Plays magical mushroom
trips that Grow all over the world, as the
entire orchestra Creates a vision of
thousands of readers dancing throughout
the universe...

And then the harp says "hi!", and the
solo violin plays a Garden full of flowers

for the reader, and then all the violins
play thousands of clones of the reader all
Dancing to the music, and then the cellos
& double basses all join in and the
thousands of clones of the reader are all
Swimming through a universe of colorful
musical notes...

And then the tuba plays the reader
discovering the ghosts of dead
comedians joking around in his attic, and
the trumpet jumps in with a bunch of
fast-fast words frolicking everywhere,
and the flute is doing some kind of dance
of monsters devouring each other...

And then the timpani drums play the
reader's brains being eaten by the reader
over a candlelight dinner, and the
reader's brains are as delicious as a
beautiful day in the park, and the
reader's brains are Growing with

symphonies & solar systems & Space
alien imaginations...

And then the solo violin plays the
reader's face Growing so many More
faces that Are growing with more faces...
And the solo cello plays the reader's face
Becoming larger & larger until the
reader's face Is bigger than the sun in
the sky, and the solo double bass plays
the reader's face Until the reader's face
is bigger than all the universe...

And the solo violin plays the reader's
Penis flying off to a fantasyland of merry
Vaginas growing everywhere, and a solo
cello plays the reader's Penis singing a
song about All one's fantasies becuming
true, and the solo double bass plays the
reader's Penis growing & growing until
the reader's Penis is growing out of the

Milky Way Galaxy and into all the other galaxies...

And as the flute plays So many crocodiles & alligators that want to eat you, the reader's Penis laughs & laughs & laughs...

And as the oboe plays a party where All the men happily exchange wives, the sun in the sky Shines upon this orgy of wiFe-eXchAnGinG-iMmaCuLaTe-cOnCepTioN with so much joy...

And the clarinet plays a thousand monkeys losing their virginity to a sexy nymphomaniac woman. This is when the reader's Vagina grows & grows until it swallows all the planets in the solar system...

(Because the reader has both a Penis & a Vagina.)

And the tuba plays the reader's Penis & the reader's Vagina dancing together...

And the harp plays the reader's Penis & the reader's Vagina searching for Peace-on-Earth together...

And then the chimes play the reader's bellybutton Getting lost in Lots of smiling similes...

And then the castanets play the reader's feet going To the crazy festival with so many other walking crazy-crazy-crazies...

And then the entire orchestra plays cRaZy-cRazY-cRaZy together, as the reader's entire body does a bunch of crazy with the crazy music...

And as the reader's ears hear all the fucking in the music, the chorus begins singing...

The chorus sings: "Summer is the time for Having sex with all the stars in the sky! Winter is the time for Jacking off all the snowmen in the park! Spring is the time for Flowers ejaculating poetry into the air!"

And then the flute starts to sing a tribute to Masturbation, and the French horn sings out a Fanatical Ooooooorgasm, and the clarinet sings with lots of Stop signs, and the trumpet sings with so much cUnNiLinGuS-cuNniLiNgUs-cUnNiLiNguS...

And then each one of the violins & cellos & double basses sings a different message to all the space aliens out there, and that all sounds like a delicious Human feast to the space aliens, it sounds like so much LSD floating the music off to a dozen fantasies, with the rhythms going Into your panties, and the rhythms Welcome the reader to Everything that is unreal, and the rhythms Create so much unreality that Everyone in the audience gets lost on other planets...

And the male singer sings: "I welcome you to the writer's brains! You & I can Summon all the beasts of all the world's fairytales together! We can bathe in All the blood flowing out of the books together!"

And the female singer sings: "I lost My virginity in the vast catacombs of Edgar Allan Poe's imagination! I found my Virginity again in the Sewers of medieval Paris! So many flying chickens for all the Zombies waiting to eat us in the park!"

And then the solo violin gets lost in a maze of Naughtiness, and the solo cello

gets lost in the maze Of tomorrow, and
the solo double bass gets lost in a maze
of All your fears...

And all the woodwinds are playing a
story of Wild animals frolicking like
Sunshine in the Darkness. And the brass
section bursts through with a bunch of
Wild words. And the timpani drums are
doing so much damage with all their
Nuclear bombs...

And the chorus sings: "Wild words that
Give you back your youth! Wild the
words That make you healthy again! Wild
the words that Love you with so much
temptation!"

And the voices of the chorus sound like
Andy Warhol being chopped into pieces
by hungry cannibals, it sounds like Cubist
Creations running all around you, all

those voices together are Eating so many holes through your face...

And then the electric guitar joins in with a bunch of Hooliganism. And the violins all join the electric guitar with a bunch of Chatter about Which musical notes are sexy and which are not. And then the ondes Martenot starts flying around with a bunch of insect sounds... The music sounds like so much Laughing cartoon characters flying around everywhere... The rhythms are so much tropical fruit that tastes delicious to the reader's ears...

And the female singer sings: "I give you my naked body with so much Disaster! I give you my sex With nuclear bombs! Nuclear bombs & sex & Crazy Charlie Chapman clones dancing everywhere!"

And the electric guitar plays executions along the wall. And the brass section joins the electric guitar with so much electric chairs laughing & laughing! And the woodwinds all throw in their Unborn babies! And the ondes Martenot is doing so much Damage to Any peace & serenity in the world that Lots of yummy happens! It's doing so much Crashing through everything conventional that Nobody even knows where their genitals are!

And the male singer sings: "I throw my body into the gutter and cover myself with raw sewage! I throw my mind into 24 hours a day of pornography & more pornography & more pornography! I sing so much pornography that I give birth to a thousand paintings with my voice!"

And the male singer's voice sounds like Laughing plastic sex dolls Sitting in royal golden chairs at the Versailles palace in France. It sounds like an erotic show in heaven. His voice sounds like so much Erotic fireworks in your butt!

And then the audience & all the musicians take a crack-cocaine break together. And the audience & musicians mingle with each other as they smoke crack cocaine.

And then the musicians get back on stage...

And the entire orchestra starts to play crack-cocaine music. Each instrument in the orchestra is playing a different crack-cocaine Fantasy. And together, all the instruments sound like a crack-cocaine Empire that's conquering the universe. It

all sounds like a crack-cocaine Bar
mitzvah with lots of Grizzly bears.

And the rhythms are the rhythms of
crack-cocaine Flying machines buzzing
around your head! And the rhythms of
the crack-cocaine music are Delicious to
the ears of all the space aliens! And all
the instruments are playing a different
crack-cocaine Message to all the bOners
in the basement! The music sounds like a
painting with Lots of erections in heaven!
The melodies are crashing & crashing
together! It all sounds like a crack-
cocaine paradise! It all sounds like a
thousand Hieronymus Bosch clones all
bouncing & bouncing all over the
auditorium as the music plays!

And the crack-cocaine chorus begins
singing: "The dancing dogs are dancing
out of all the Vaginas of the convent! Our

ears are floating into the Wilds of the Apocalypse! And the Fish in your brains are jumping out into the air and devouring everyone!"

And the crack-cocaine audience sings back to the chorus: "We love crack-cocaine! We love fucking domesticated animals in the legislative & executive & judicial branches of the government! We love jizzying our art all over the faces of the founding fathers of our Lovely country!"

And the crack-cocaine chorus sings back to the audience: "Soon, the Giant spiders will be crawling into our imaginations and devouring our brains! And after that, the wild animals will cum and play us some wine & cheese music! And that's why we love you! We love you with so much Vietnam War!"

And the audience sings back to the chorus: "We love you too! We love you with so much Paradise of the STDs in between our legs, and we wish to give our paradise to you! Our love for you is So full of falling bombs & flying bullets!"

And the chorus sings back to the audience: "We would love you in our stomachs! We will love you with so much cannibalism! Cannibalism is the most divine music!"

And then the male singer sings in praise of crack-cocaine: "Crack-cocaine is the humongous hairy God testicles in your wet dreams! Crack-cocaine will save us with so much Glory hallelujah space alien buttocks! Crack-cocaine is the Savior!"

And then the female singer sings in praise of crack-cocaine: "Praise crack-cocaine for the iambic pentameter in our buttholes! Praise the Lord for giving us crack-cocaine! Now let us pray for the gods of graffiti art to create us some Heavenly murals of sin!"

And then the audience sings in praise of crack-cocaine: "We love so much the incest growing & growing in all the neighborhoods of all the cities! And We love the Preacher with his Penis preaching so much Spermatozoa! The preacher's Penis is a gift to all of you!"

And then the solo violin plays a crack-cocaine Lullaby. And the solo cello plays so much crack-cocaine Words growing all over the Walls. And the solo double bass is doing so much crack-cocaine, that his music sounds like Millions of devils fornicating with the musical notes...

And then the woodwinds play so much crack-cocaine! And the woodwinds play so much Delicious sky for all the penguins to eat! And it all sounds like God picking his nose with so much musical Rhythms! It's so much crack-cocaine rhythms that You begin eating your own thoughts! It's so many melodies of crack-cocaine, that You simultaneously jump out of thousands of paintings in all the world's art museums!

And then the brass section plays a Hurricane of crack-cocaine. It's a flotilla of hundreds of flying toilets! It's so much crack-cocaine music that Jesus falls to his knees and Performs fellatio on Charles Manson!

And the timpani drums are playing so Many thrills & adventures of crack-cocaine! It sounds like the booming Conquering Empire of crack-cocaine! It's all the booming-booming crack-cocaine drums going to all the delicious places in your mind! Drums & more drums going booming-booming yippee! So much booming-booming crack-cocaine music! It's absolutely glorious with crack-cocaine!

And then the ondes Martenot flies everywhere with so much crack-cocaine! It's so much crack-cocaine flying music that You have a heart attack! The ondes Martenot sounding like all the Glorious heart attacks of crack-cocaine! The ondes Martenot sounding like so Much history eating through your body!

And then the entire orchestra plays together in the Religious spirits of crack-cocaine! It's a crack-cocaine extravaganza! It's a crack-cocaine extravaganza of Religious Revelation music played on top of a rock mountain of Crack! Music filling your ears with so much Hallucinations! So much crack-cocaine music filling your ears that All the insane asylums of the world are suddenly inside your head!

And then the male singer sings: "I hereby declare that transvestite kangaroos are the salvation of our nation!"

And the female singer sings: "And I hereby declare that transvestite kangaroos make my Pussy as wet as the Mediterranean Sea!"

And the chorus sings: "And we hereby declare that the children shall be eaten by the puppies, and the founding fathers of our nation will be eaten by the gargoyles flying around, and the priests & preachers will be eaten by God!"

And the audience sings: "Testicles to all the nuns in Our wet dreams! Nun Pussy to all the koala bears bouncing up-&-down the Musical scales! The ants crawling from some Salvador Dali painting to Your living room are all whispering their hallucinations to us!"

And crack addicts throughout the world sing together: "We are the Strawberry sinners Who will be partying with you inside your grave! We are the Children of Rainbows! Tomorrow the yeast infections of The Land of Oz will percolate & percolate their extreme colors all over the walls of the world!"

And then the entire orchestra plays a Thousand walls full of graffiti-art together. And the ondes Martenot flies around again with so much Skin-burning-off-your-body music! It's so many rhythms of words burning throughout your neighborhood! It's so Many delicious musical notes Down your throat! It's so many Flying saucers flying into your ears!

And then the flute plays a man chopping off his own limbs...

And the male singer begins laughing & laughing...

And the clarinet plays a lot of Laughing hyenas gobbling each other up...

And the female singer begins laughing & laughing...

And the timpani drums do lots of Words crashing through everything...

And both the male singer & the female singer begin laughing & laughing. And as the woodwinds all play a bunch of laughter, the male singer & female singer laugh and laugh like the clouds flowing over your head, they laugh and laugh like space alien brains being barbecued in your backyard, they laugh and laugh like Madmen burning in the fires of your brains...

And then the entire brass section begins playing a bunch of laughter. And the brass section sounds like all the trees uprooting themselves and walking towards the Infinity of a never-ending math equation, it sounds like Your best friend grabbing a shotgun and putting it into his mouth, and it sounds like Billions of people jumping into a burning bonfire one-by-one...

And then the entire chorus begins laughing. They're laughing & singing at the same time... And it sounds like an alcoholic drinking himself into an

apocalyptic heaven on the day he dies,
and it sounds like Two serial killers
admiring each other from different sides
of the universe, and it sounds like Your
mother's naked body beckoning you to
things that...

And then the solo violin plays sadness.
And the sadness sounds like a sad man
laughing all the way to the cemetery.
The sadness sounds like a sad woman
laughing all the way Back to her
childhood. The sadness sounds like so
much Laughter in the walls...

And the solo cello & solo double bass join
the solo violin, and the three strings
together sound like so much sadness,
and all the sadness sounds like
Happiness being put into a boiling pot of
Human body parts, it's so much sadness

that Your eyeballs start searching for other planets to live on...

And then each member of the entire string section plays their own sadness, and it's a Thousand smiling faces of sadness, It all sounds like Your hands falling off from too much masturbation, it all sounds like a bOiLiNg-bOiLinG-citY of sadness. Sadness and more sadness and more sadness...

But then the timpani drums begin playing a bunch of destruction. And it all sounds like a Flying wrecking ball of destruction. It sounds like People chopping off their own heads, and dancing their headless bodies across the Sentences that keep dashing across these pages! So much iNcOmPreHenSibLe-eXplOdiNg-aNgeR coming from the timpani drums!

And then the brass section & woodwinds play so much panic! Panic and more panic and more panic sounding like so much Musical avalanches going Berserk inside of you! The whole woodwinds section sounding like Spermatozoa flying everywhere. The brass section sounding like a thousand wild animals that want to devour you in your dreams tonight...

And the chorus sings: "What ding-a-lings are we Flying with now? When will the Rabies take effect? How much more Psycho ferris wheel of emotions until We collapse?"

But then the orchestra becomes happy again! The entire orchestra playing so much happiness! It's the happiness of Your three testicles singing to you of Paradise all night long! It's the happiness of Losing your brains to a space alien every day! The music sounds like the happiness of castration & more castration & more castration! The music sounds like People exchanging body parts with space aliens...

And then the flute player starts to walk offstage and through the audience as he plays Human blood dripping on all the planets... And the clarinet player follows the flute player off the stage and into the audience, as the clarinet plays a bunch of Jesus Christ clones on thousands of crosses all laughing & laughing. And the bassoon & the oboe also walk out into the audience, and they're playing a bunch of Romantic-beautiful-outhouses together.

And then the trumpet also leaves the stage and walks out into the audience, and the trumpet is So happy with

Siamese twins chopping each other up with chainsaws! The trumpet is Throwing out exclamation points of Wonderful diseases! The trumpet Is so overwhelming with so many wonderful diseases that You become infected with everything!

And the French horn walks offstage after the trumpet, and the French horn player stands amongst the audience playing so much Beautiful elegant French nouveau whorehouses, He's playing so much Massive amounts of elegant French nouveau jizz, He's playing a lot of Insanity going out for a walk...

And the tuba follows the French horn into the audience, and the tuba is playing a hilarious Comedy about Everyone exchanging faces with each other, the tuba is playing so much funny Jokes that everybody is laughing like Rats & cockroaches fornicating on spaceships, the tuba is playing laughter and more laughter...

And then the male singer follows the tuba as the male singer sings: "Let's laugh while we die! Let's laugh while we kill! Let's laugh while We eat our own body organs!"

And the female singer follows the male singer, and the female singer sings: "Let's cry while we Stab our eyes into the mirror all day long! Let's tear our own eyes out while we Dance across fields of corpses! Let's attack the silence with endless screams!"

And then the entire chorus follows, and walks out into the audience, and the chorus sings: "Let's have a nuclear war with so much Sugar & nice! Let's die at the hands of artificial intelligence while we Create one last poem that will triumph with all humanity! Let's play hide & seek amongst the Statues of our ancestors!"

And then the entire audience & the entire chorus sing together: "Let's blastoff to the Other side of Reality! Let's eat all the Buildings! Let's drink & drink until Our bodies are bleeding with Joy!"

And then the ondes Martenot starts playing All the animals of the planet Earth flying around the auditorium. The ondes Martenot starts creating so much Exotic things that never existed before. It sounds as if Death is flying around the room as the ondes Martenot plays & plays & plays...

And then the harp & timpani drums & vibes all start floating in the air of the

auditorium. And together, the harp &
timpani drums & vibes are playing so
much End-of-the-world smashing into
the beginning-of-the-world, they're
playing so much Sexy-sexy Worms that
the reader Ignites himself on fire, they're
playing So many musical notes on fire
that all your memories begin burning
down...

And the ondes Martenot goes wild again!
And the ondes Martenot sounds like All
the testicles on the planet Earth dingling
& dingling & dingling, it sounds like
Everybody's ears is being drenched with
The sounds of the impossible, and the
sound vibrates with so much Hunger!

And the audience sings: "The end is here
with so Many smiling grim reapers
standing in front of us! The ending of this
book will eat us!"